THE FOLIATE HEAD

THE FOLIATE HEAD

Marly Youmans

Stanza

To Clive Hicks-Jenkins

THE FOLIATE HEAD
Marly Youmans

Images by Clive Hicks-Jenkins

First Edition

ISBN 978-1-84863-460-2

Design and layout by Andrew Wakelin
Printed and bound in England by
TJ International Ltd, Padstow, Cornwall

Stanza Press
an imprint of PS Publishing
Grosvenor House
1 New Road
Hornsea
East Yorkshire HU18 1PG
United Kingdom

editor@pspublishing.co.uk
www.pspublishing.co.uk

Contents

POWERS

In the Shadow of the Jasmine

"in the shade—the eternal jasmine's—
with immaculate joy."
Wasyl Barka, *The Mad Woman*

As white as jasmine though more crystalline,
The snow goes on for miles around the house
Under a freighted, leaning sky of ice.
So it has been for months—first the river
Flowing choppily between us and, next,
Torrential time, widening the spaces.
Then came the soft relentlessness of snow.
At first I thought one second was enough
To alter us forever and bereave
My soul of you—and so it was—but soon
Your face went slipping through my memory
Like water that no human hands can hold
Until I ran along the banks of death,
Stumbling, cutting my feet, calling your name,
And there I glimpsed the shade of you, not torn
In pieces by mad terror's strike .... To think,
They've named me mad who had divinest sense
Of love for you that would not ebb and die
As others wished, as others would commend!
I knew your voice, your body wavering
As if in ancient glass—you steadied, were
A vision of full-bodied soul, my love,
Who elsewhere lay in fragments in the grave,
And there along the shrapnel-edge of death,
We made the only vows we'll ever have,
To walk past time into the jasmine shade
Where fragrance may be music, where our love
May fuse with light, where we're not as we were.

At night my sheets are white as miles of snow;
My body, restless, aches for what is not,
And when I sleep my dreams are jasmine-lit.
I wander in the moonlight, break the stems
Of closed-up jasmine flowers just at dawn
And make them into tea. Sun's corolla
Transforms into a single jessamine.

Above your bones I draw in snow a bloom
That glints as if it were a diamond brooch—
A scentless thing with dust at every heart
Of every flake of snow. No matter how
Broken, each crystal star is beautiful,
Fallen from perfection into a world
Infinitely precious, infinitely
Small against the dark and galaxies.
My love, my love, there is no terror here
But only grief that passes and a joy
I cannot share, these stars upon my skin.
I bend to taste the snow, and it is sweet.

Clock of the Moon and Stars

O, clock of the silver moon and stars, stop
This incessant trickling and spilling in chimes;
Hasn't there been enough of singing—choir
At its struggles, *Magnum Mysterium*
Going backward and forward and inside out,
The women trilling over mops as the doors
Fly open and the suds freeze on the snow,
The poor child with its shrill demanding song
That called the spirits to take possession?
Hasn't there been enough of dropping
The quarter hours and the whole in chimes?

You harry me, you remind me of much,
O clock of the moon and stars: the silvery
Mysteries and the past and the damned child
Hurtled to hell in a carriage of flame.

Lumen Hour

Ankle-deep, I stand in lapping waves,
An enormous disk of sunlit water
—Bankless, yet staying a perfect circle—
To my left fed by the silvery river,
Waters raveled wide like unbraided hair.
Elsewhere are fell, wondrous niagaras,
Curved like threaded bows too long for any
Mortal hand to bend and make obey.
Here and there, geysers of mist catch light,
Fine rainbowed flarings, and above are more
Bows hanging in the clouds like promises
Or threats that what is strung may be of use
To one with arms to bend immortal bows.
Women clamber over rocks and reach me,
And so I ask the way—there's only one,
The women tell me. All is as I guessed.

That Which Snatches

Vulture-like, the harpies wheel on updrafts
Or settle in the grove of wind-whipped trees,
Their small, secretive faces looking out
Without sign of interest or passion,
As pinched and harsh as soul heads on a stone
Propped up by mourning Puritans on land
Unused to buried bone: winged skulls that glare.
One is singing, *Turn away, my bonnie,*
Turn away home, and yet there is nowhere
To turn, no home when such weird sisters sing.
In Cretan caves they hang like ungroomed bats,
Letting locks hang, letting the lice parade,
Their molting feathers like some nightmare bed
Where no man fancies lying—that's a truth
That galls, for only breeze that glances here
And there and then is gone could bear to kiss
Their shriveled, wicked purse of privacies.

Bedraggled, murderous, entirely foul ...
If they had hands, the fingers would be small,
As leathery as paws for throwing scat
At queens or prophets. No respect, no cheer,
No proper sentiment for the flawless
Horses of Achilles, their own offspring,
That wept to smell the battle-scent of death.
No sisterly devotion to Iris
Tricked out in sunstruck iridescent drops.

They'll shriek the dawn awake and howl for flesh,
Heraldic frights so ignorant of evil
They could be us—so self-absorbed, so free.
On branches in the bleeding wood of souls,

They shift their talons, sigh in sleep like doves,
Dreaming of men like birds of paradise,
Of leaf-winged forests tumbling in a storm,
The phoenix burning on her nest of myrrh
Who found this harpied world worth dying for.

Artifact

To me, the *Magical Museum*'s prize
Looked made from barley-twists of glass, not horn,
Shadow-infiltrated and streaked with dyes.
A grimy card read "shard of unicorn."

When someone has no faith, who knows what pulls?
An impulse seized my hand; I stole the rod.
Could it be signpost to impossibles?
This way to fairies, demons, throne of God?

Once rinsed, its substance flared and seemed to bless
As words made promises within two minds:
When virgin flesh compels my love and binds,
We are the proof of this world's loveliness ...

> *O ravished dream, now grace has fled, what horn*
> *Can heal the ways the globe and we are torn?*

To Make Much of Time

Why must you fritter, twitter, play
And want fresh hours to the day?
Bend now, bend now to the work
That sings your name—or will you hark
Forever to what others do,
Even when less fraught than you
With gifts a fairy christening
Might envy? Did an angel wing
Disturb the air above your face,
Fanning those cradled silks and lace?
Yet soon enough the years fly on,
Turn gold silver, dandelion
Suns to gray-gilt clocks of hours...
And your easy, springing powers
Will sink to dusk and dust, and wink
Away, like sun over the brink
Of Earth: what mind conceives, let hands
Enact and make, let spirit lands
And human lands unite in tale
And image—let new light prevail
Against the armies of the dark,
And be the wakened, daybreak lark.

The Elder Race

They had a flair for fountain-smithery,
So that the tears flew up in joy like drops
Ascending to a realm of peace, to stand
Prismatic—as if magical—on air
Before the dazzling strings collapsed in stars
Inside a marble basin ... The cogs and wheels,
The tiny valves that shot apart when steam
Flashed and geysered, whistling through the gas-pipes
To whirl the figures by a silver lake
To dancing: what gilt-loveliness they were,
Those works of nimbleness. Such simple things
As ball or box approached the marvelous;
It tugged the heart to see the latticed spheres
In spheres, the leaf-shaped latch, the hidden drawer—
Its subtle, crafty mechanism sunk
Deeper than a hand could find by groping.

I wonder now if they disliked our arts,
Those cheaper, stillborn copies of their works
That seemed to glint in mockery of craft
And creation at every peddler's stall.
Perhaps they never noticed what we hatched:
Why should an eye alight on mounds of straw
When fine-spun gold makes flourishes on air?
They always seemed on verge of vanishing—
A flash of profile lost in market crowds,
A glim-lit form receding over waves,
A figure moving off through twilit trees.
I used to hear them singing as they crossed
The stile beside my father's meadowland,
Their voices sweet, their native language strange,
And I would run outside to watch them pass,
Afraid of gammer-gossip and yet drawn.

One fall they were less common in our towns—
Swell jettison! crowed local shopkeepers,
Although for several years the prices sailed
Cloud-high wherever well-smithed goods were hawked.
Their paths of chalk that glowed on lunar nights
Began to melt away, as if trails poured
From salt were yielding to the autumn rains,
Withdrawing like the end of mystery.
Though I was young, I still recall the hour
I glimpsed the last of them in snowy woods,
The fierceness in his eyes that branded me
As surely as if glances could be coal.
He nodded, seemed to vanish in the hill,
And though I knocked, no answer was returned.
He must have spied some artful gift in me
To leave a chest of tools beside my door
With gold and silver wire and beveled gems,
That I will work despite my ignorance
And out of longing for their kind and grief.

The Substance

Fine as a ring-stole drawn through a hoop
Of gold, but crimped and burned
And almost ruined by some fire
Long ago, far away—
Glimmering like abalone,
Moody and beautiful.

Some things persist as mystery,
No matter how we seek
A raveling, no matter how
We vaunt, no matter how—
Slanting above our lifted faces
Like rain shot through by sun.

The Sheaf of Wheat

Subtle, suffused light in the sheaf of grain
Is pale gold that's almost silver,
Like, in a certain leaning light, the rain,
Slender arrows from a quiver

Of cloud: the reign of light is piercing, sharp,
And I am a Saint Sebastian,
A pincushion, a hedgehog, or a harp
Of many strings—belated bastion

Of love and golden fire. The pavement says
Exultemus in nomine...
The stained glass window catches at the rays
Of light, and all is comedy,

Play with happy endings, bright upwelling
Worlds away from getting, selling.

Scout Ceremony

Old choices made are all around—
Across the way, the hanging ground,

Above, the mansions on the ridge,
And underfoot, the hand-laid bridge.

The trees all luminous with snow,
The flaming arrow on the bow,

The solemn older boys who cross
The crenellated bridge and foss

Between the worlds, while arcs of fire
Make images of heart's desire:

This cobbled-up mythology,
This arrow's blaze of purity—

The animals with human speech,
The four-direction winds that teach

The west of dark, the east of light,
The compass of the soul's delight

Surprise us with a note of power
That lingers past the meeting hour.

The Stone Court

I didn't meet the terror's lightning-strike,
Jag-necked Medusa whom the painters praise
With heads that show a severed life can prick
Its serpent hair to hissing, howl the mouth
In everlasting *No!* against the world:
My eyes were dwelling on the stranger's eyes
Reflected from the hero's godborn shield—
Long-throated head, the twist of gleaming hair,
The moony skin as luminous as pearl.
I hadn't known that I was beautiful.
A horse that sprang from blood unshipped its wings ...
The hero thumped Medusa's head in a bag,
Chucked it across his shoulder, and flew away.
My mother's brother, come to plead a cause,
Stiff with anger ... I kissed his limestone cheek,
Was glad of wine and barley flatbreads tucked
Inside a cloth, and thieved the king's own knife—
He'd have no further clasp on weaponry
But would forever claw a fleaborn itch
Beneath a cloak of stone. A tippler's mouth
Was plugged, a snatched caress was tombed in rock:
The figures looked too real: impossible,
A little corny, certainly not art
Or worth my grief. I hardly felt the loss
Just then, drifting in the cloud of knowledge
That was my youth, a shield around my limbs,
Though floating motes once dust were adamant
To sting my face to tears. I threaded paths
Between arrested courtesies of court
And stared as dazzle of a shield and horse
Made starfalls retrograde. Though sapphire sky
Slanted a jeweled lid above the stones,
I never feared but walked a thousand steps
Before the world began to yield to green.

I bore a light-drenched memory of me,
A soft and yielding vision, stream of flame
Or water welling in a fresh-dug pit,
And slowly realized the morning's truth:
The power of my gaze protected me.
The island's edge came curling to my feet;
I walked in brightness like a springtime sun,
Carrying myself as one who witnessed
The dangers burning from a woman's face.
I bore myself like glory in a cloud
As I moved swiftly over hills to home,
Goatherds called me by the name of *Ceres*
And begged me make the ground grow deep with grass,
And country people knotted near the path
To see the goddess green the early fields.
Though all the flame was vigor of my youth
And borrowed magic of a fearsome sight,
I came in after-years to meditate
How I alone escaped the pitiless
And wondered that the innocence of youth
And joy could blunt the edge of brute demand,
Declaring by mere thoughtless going-on
That life was far too vigorous to end.

Transfiguration

Here are three sleepers on a mountaintop,
And here's a man awake beneath the sky—
Coinlike, the moonshine rims the profiled head.
And yet not moon but glimmerings of fire
That strengthen, shine like candlelight through snow
Until the face, the hands, and raiment seethe:
His shape of light is wholly beautiful
And useless with the uselessness of art
That's meant for nothing but the beautiful,
That does nothing but transform utterly
And has no message to deliver us
But is the revelation of itself.

Down in the gulf, a demon-raptured boy
Makes manifest the fallen world with howls.

Interregnum

You are alone inside the dark,
Your head is bent as if in prayer ...
For unwashed weeks you have been still,
So still, that eyes may rest and heal.
Sometimes your head is bent in prayer
But always it is bent and yields
To what the others say is best.
Bereft until someone appears,
Husband or friend: so you have learned
Who is a friend and who is not.
The knot of marriage, will it hold
Against such cumberings as these?
Sometimes the muse is there to sing,
Sometimes *le moi profond* awakes
To feel, exquisitely, its pain,
Dark stars of hopelessness or hope,
Outlandish modes of forsaking,
The pen grown weighty in your hand,
The thrust, the minnow-dart of words
Congealed and dammed above the stream.

And now you'll drowse as Christmas comes
And Twelfth Night goes in gaiety
This year for others, not for you.
Old Winter rules your fallen world
And lets the snowflakes bridal earth,
The icicles collect in crowns,
And all your powers curl in sleep—
This is the Advent of your sight.
Still wait inside the dark for light.

The Great Frost

Now comes her winter, when the roads are choked
With snow and all the staring ways go blind.
Though she's no bird, the tower points upward
From sheets of windswept ice—below, the fish
And monster hang suspended in the lake.
At cold distance, the villagers are glimpsed,
Each as alone as she, each rampart-walled
With battlements of January snow ...
The rainy season seems so long away,
And now with song she tries to shatter floes
That pour from roofs and seal against the ground
Until no portals open to the world.

Her words mean violence to the glacial town,
And craze with hairline faults the spill of glass
That helmets home, makes stirring treacherous.
She bends to creation despite a hush
That sinks inside the blue titanic dusk.

The fool! The village idiot! No tears,
She cries no silly tears. Poor vernal loon,
Her children lie exposed upon the hill,
And still she keeps on singing as if soon
Those jailed in crystal will break into song.

"I Heard Their Wings Like the Sound of Many Waters"

In the dark, in the deeps of the night that are
Crevasses of a sea, I heard their wings.
I heard the trickling of tiny feathers
With their hairs out like milkweed parachutes
Floating idly on the summer air,
I heard the curl and splash, the thunderbolts
Of pinions, the rapids and rattle of shafts—
Heard Niagara sweep the barreled woman
And shove her under water for three days,
I heard a jar of fragrance spill its waves
As a lone figure poured out all she could,
Heard the sky's bronze-colored raindrops scatter
On corrugated roofs and tops of wells,
I heard the water-devil whirligigs,
I heard an awesome silence when the wings
Held still, upright as flowers in a vase,
And when I turned to see why they had stilled,
Then what I saw was likenesses to star
Imprisoned in a form of marble flesh,
With a face like lightning-fires and aura
Trembling like a rainbow on the shoulders,
But all the else I saw was unlikeness
That bent me like a bow until my brow
Was pressed against the minerals of earth,
And when I gasped at air, I tasted gold.

THE BOOK OF YSTWYTH

In honor of the 60th birthday retrospective
of artist Clive Hicks-Jenkins.

The Blue Marches

"This early painterly approach to objects can be seen in
Journey's End, *the little still-life/landscape painting of*
my dad's tea mug standing in front of Tretower Castle."
Clive Hicks-Jenkins

There's nothing here bejeweled with twig and flower,
No wolfish fur that burns as if a kiln
Had been flung wide to let in sprays of salt,
And most of all, no story, wings, or saint.
Instead there is the seepage of a blue
Not twilight: low, continual dim glow
Dispersed from borderlands beyond this world.

So here is landscape as the stillest life,
So here is still life hunkered in the grass,
Estranged from lamplit houses, grown outscale.
There's nothing here but cup and keep and tree,
And tree resembles keep, and keep is tree
Truncated—cup is stump of leaning tree.

No teller yet, unless the tale be one
Older than the famed white book of Rhydderch,
Older than the red of Hergest, older
By far than these… Fetch me a magic fruit
So I can taste its glistening cells and gulp
The stubborn words that linger out of reach.

In blueing light, a father's mug might be
The grail, might be Welsh cauldron, wombed with life,
Might over-brim with death-drink, colorless.
There's nothing but a shadow in the cup!
Its clipper ship in sail is doldrum-glazed,
Forgets the fragrance of darjeeling seas.

The motte, a mound of good Welsh earth, was his,
As was the tower vacant to the sky,
The kingdom known as Powys long ago,
And all the rainy borderland of blue—
All things that flee and hide in borderlands
Between the earth and sky belonged to him.

But now he has passed through that realm of dreams
And left you wondering by hills of earth,
And long you'll muse, and long you'll meditate
And never understand the world you brushed
Across that sheet of paper: world where tree
Is keep, and keep is tree, and cup can loom
As high as high Tretower or a tree.

Journey's End, 1999

Hermitry

Sunday when the bells
Were ringing, I dreamed a fine,
High singing in air—

An oval of leaves
Aspired, became cloud. I cried
To the Lord, "Spare me

From maiden-doom, flesh
Conflagrate in marriage-bed,"
And touched the little

Apples of my breasts
And braids that said I was not
Mine, nor Christ's alone.

They never warned me
That God's reply is direful,
Unlike anything.

I slipped into sleep
Within sleep, dreamed the swollen
Womb of an oak tree,

My veins suckling sap ...
A portal slit allowed light,
Dilated, clasped head

And shoulder: I eased
Like a tender flower-bud
From the lips of tree,

Below a Venus
Mound of leaves—a boy so new
In his second birth,

He scarcely marked day's
Magic cauldron, its wildfire
Breaking in the skies,

The blast of power
Or the exoskeleton
That armed the angel

Whose eyes glanced away,
A delicate intrusion:
The hands offered life

Guised as *bara brith*
That in another instant
The boy took and ate.

The Man Who Lived in a Tree, 2003-4

Master Jug and Lady Candle Stick

With hands on hips and foliate attire,
    The candlestick is all umbrageousness,
A shady lady who has stripped the trees
    At upper right to flock her dress with leaves,
A woman apt to give or take offense,
    Set resolute beside the one-armed jug.
The wide blue boat of hat upholds a stub
    With candlewick to warn his waters off—
She'll have no wild outpourings of his love,
    No boarding of the levees of her skirts.
She doesn't know that he, entrenched in peace,
    Is only musing on the color blue
And how he can by rounding clasp the sea
    Until his wheel-turned soul grows chasmal-deep.
Impaled upon a thorn, the little fish
    At lower right perceives what she cannot
And dreams cloud-cuckoo lands below the waves—
    Will get there just as soon as Master Jug
Can gather all the seas inside himself,
    Enspelling blue chimeric revery.

The Blue Jug, 2006

Dear Peregrine,

You said "phantasmagoria" and asked
Just how such things happen, how my life changed,
And how I, burning, could embrace the flame
Like Daniel striding, singing in the threads
Of windblown fire that seemed but harvest wheat,
The summer color of a lion's pelt ...

My making was a strangeness to the world,
Announced by angel messenger: *Hervé*
Would be devoted to the Lord. The two
Predestined as my parents met and matched
And parted in a dream of holiness.
My mother prayed my eyes be undeceived.
My father prayed me visions sent from God.
They made a child the messenger foretold.

I was a little boy immured in night,
A land where Rivanone ran quicksilver
Through shade of trees, my mother Rivanone,
Where father meant a voice to say or chant
That shook the boughs and lingered by the throne
Of distant kings: Hyvarnian the bard,
Who bade me be like him. What did I know,
A blind small boy for whom no one looked king,
And all was trees with leaves of onyx skin
That rustled with the telling of my tales,
And all was stream that whispered Rivanone?

Then came my frolic, curl-tailed dog that danced
Around my feet and chased the leaves with joy
And skimmed his name in barks across the stream.
I spired aloft, a sapling in the woods,
And every day I learned new tales and songs
And combed the waves of singing Rivanone.

Some say that forests are best cleansed by fire,
That plants upfling their forms as if renewed
When wildfire crackles by—one day a burst
Of sun fell down from heaven to my face.
I swam inside its waterfalls of light,
Sluiced and rinsed by bonfire's streaming petals,
Until I sensed with second sight the face
That hides itself within a glowing tree.
So then I saw, though dimly, stems of word
And waves of syllables, as if the monks
Had made the world a dark calligraphy
To tell me how all things were made of word
That issued burning from the mouth of God.

The wolf was tangled up with what I knew—
Scathe-mouthed, he rushed to scoop my little dog
And made a tidbit of his dainty shape
Before he slammed between my empty arms.
I somehow knew the wildfire of his fur
Was kindled from the tinder of the words,
And all the world was innocent of guile.
The more he set a bracelet of his teeth
Around my arm, the more I sang out love
To rock the earth and unearth rock, to read
The leaf, the stream, the blind fantastic world
Until the forest flashed almighty light.

And now if I should grieve the dark no more,
If I should whoop and carol to the boles,
The wolf my partner in a fearsome dance,
My life phantasmagoria of joy,
Then do not pity me, for I have read
The writing on the walls of blind-eyed earth,
And do not blame the wolf for anything,
For God Almighty, bard above all bards,

Has crowned his head with glory like a saint's
And set the words of wildfire in his fur.

Pax tecum,
Hervé

Furious Embrace, 2007

Catriona's Plate

1. Woman as Delft

Up center, down center, and apron, she
Is dominating stage and drops of scenery:
Her flower-painted presence calls the eye
To fly old walls of fieldstone, magically restored,
Fish-skeletons of branches tipped with green,
And pilgrim's scallop shell that crowns proscenium.

Why is her stageset kingdom painted blue
Like sky or sea? Is she to sail somewhere through cloud
Or ocean? Must she be eternally
Moored at harbor, freighted with ripe pomegranates?

Ynysypandy Slate Mill – Toy Theatre with
Delft Plate and Pomegranates, 2004

2. Delft as Memento Mori

Earthly all is dangerous to china—
Blunted seal-brown shapes of cliffs, then plunging absence.
The sea goes dark with something like a thought.
St. Govan's little oratory is unseen,
As secret in the earth as was the bell
That pirates stole and angels thrust inside a stone.

The Delft's as lovely-fragile as before,
But someone's tasted pomegranates snug with seed:
The plate is vacant. Sprigs of sea thrift kiss
The lip in ceding to the wind's invisibles.

Delft Plate and Sea Thrift, St. Govan's Head, 2005

THE GREEN WORLD

Puck in Spring

Now the catamount will scream,
Now the bears awake from dream
That the winter's night prolongs
Till the ice dissolves in songs.
Now the daybreak fires the mist
By the mountain ridges kissed.
While the crocus blossoms yield,
Opening along the field.
Now it is the hour in spring
When the jetting sap will bring
Fresh desire to boy and girl
Waking to a brighter world.
And the fairies hunting shade,
Finding meadow grass arrayed
With the bloom of early bells,
Creep inside the fragrant cells.
Now in clearing, vale, and slope,
All the land is drunk with hope—
In the ancient greening weald,
Now is loosed what once was sealed.
Why, the very mountains reel
At the turning of the wheel.

Self-portrait as Dryad, no. 7

The golden haze around these whips of limbs
Is glistening, awakening to light
Within retreating clouds—embattled fire
That melts the snow and pellmell sends the sky
To run in ditches near the highway's edge.

My God, I am no witch to suffer so—
Who tied me to this stake that frosts my skin?
Who makes me tremble with his solar heat?
Who takes my voice and shakes the syllables
Until I speak in otherworldly tongues?

Dear Christ, the world is aching in its grave,
And can I bear another spring-time thaw?
O Willow, Willow, I uncurl to let
The bite and simmer of this raking gold
Explode in leaves—green eyes that weep for me,
My harrowed hell, my star-enkindled tree.

The Foliate Head

Peering from medieval churches,
Dressed in leaves of ash and birches,

Camperdown elm and English oak,
Doghobble, sassafras, and poke,

Here winks the sprite who can transcend
His yearly death, for whom no end

Can be unless by our misdeed.
His verdant woman bleeds to breed

A world of leaves, his phoenix-pet
Cries cockerel against regret,

Remorse, and all that's passed away
While crowing-in triumphant day.

The green man's lodge is budding wood,
His roofbeam's resurrection rood,

The axis mundi staking cloud
To earth and realms below the shroud.

The roulette balls fly round the sun,
The spiral years are never done ...

Within my dreams, he's young and lithe,
Unheeding of the reaper's scythe,

But when I meet him in the park,
He's changed his guise from light to dark;

I go to grasp his creaking hands
And find him dressed in swaddling bands.

The Magnolia Girl

She climbed the great magnolia tree
To learn the ways of bird and bee,

And there the Prince of Darkness came
To tempt her with delicious shame.

He bore her up and bore her down,
He let her try his royal crown

While leaves went clattering-a-clack
Like gossips warning at her back.

A burst of starlight from his face,
His every move a sigh of grace—

Could you resist his lightsome wiles,
Or stop the arrows of his smiles?

What was a tendency to hiss
When set beside a glowing kiss?

In long-ago and far-away,
She danced her dance the livelong day—

She showed him all her naked skin,
And what they did was mortal sin.

When boredom dulled his passion's rage,
The Serpent Prince desired a cage;

He jailed her in the blooming tree
And spread a lie that she was free.

Addicted to the streaming light
From which her lover once took flight,

She now repents those leisure hours
Misspent among magnolia flowers.

Red Leaves in Green

Than-bauk

Earthmother's dressed in leaves—
Early Autumn weaves red
Into sleeves of green.

But what of you,
Spring girl who came
To woo high Holygrove

(With gifts—cloud grass
And lake-worn glass) where
Fairies pass to Otherworlds?

Red-flecked sleeves, unearthly trees ...
The question flees away ...
Earthmother sees no girl ...

Nothing but forest's green
Stippled with keen lances,
Blood-reds between aging leaves.

Green Wednesday

He made a mask, he made a mask
Of his dear father, O!
He made it gold, made a father
All leafed with glister, O!

He fed its light to summer's king,
Jack of the Greenwood, O!
Whose wicker frame was sprangled green—
The light, the oak leaf, O!

The wildwood men were high as trees
And daubed in leaf-meal, O!
The gold-fired mask of the Father
Made glints and spangles, O!

The streaming greens poured merrily
Through Hastings roadways, O!
A father's face reborn shone young,
Smiling and leafy, O!

The mask maker was set apart
From wodwo maskers, O!
Till horn-hard palms of wild men struck
His brow with green dye, O!

Then sprigs and leafy wands uncurled
From out his mind's cage, O!
Maker and masker, green and wick–
Springflame returning, O!

Mirror Tree, Tree Mirror

The branch that fires the bloom,
The twigs that trap the moon,
The rind that jails the core,
The cells that drink the air,
The bole that lifts the sky,
The hole that shades the hive,
The knot that tugs the grain,
The scar that seals the pain,
The gall that mars the skin,
The leaf that eats the sun.

The sun that eats the leaf,
The skin that mars the gall,
The pain that seals the scar,
The grain that tugs the knot,
The hive that shades the hole,
The sky that lifts the bole,
The air that drinks the cells,
The core that jails the rind,
The moon that traps the twigs,
The bloom that fires the branch.

"Because I Pass, I Pass,
While Dreams Remain"
After Kathleen Raine

Who was it whispered in my dream?
The dream hour's angel whispered in my ear
    As pulse of sea made echoings.

What foxes bolted through the storm?
Wild longings for one man's unravished heart,
    Curses that rebounded: on me.

Whose hand the hand that gave the rose?
A hand from out eternities of sand—
    Saharas sifting through the glass.

And whose the quiet leaf that fell?
I was the leaf that ate the dancing sun.
    Mine the green fire and yellowing.

And how should you remember me?
How to tell me from the bird, the sea,
    The rising fountain in the tree?

Wielding the Tree Finder

Do you ramble the ground—are you a tree and yet a forest,
    does your great bulk blossom in one night
    like an elephant singing a love-song to the moon,
    do you transform to a reservoir for water and stars,
    do you grow hollow for whistling,
    do you become an ossuary,
    do you hold African mummies in your heart,
    are you *baobab*?

Were you sacred to healers and priests who haunted oak groves,
    golden shoulder pins on their woven garments,
    your parasite branches in their hands
    —the raspberry girl slaughtered, seeds between her teeth—
    were you sharpened to a Norseman's spearpoint,
    did your mischief kill a god, fairest of the Aesir,
    do you draw warmth of kisses to an orb of leaves,
    are you *mistletoe*?

Are the rosy pastors and the bulbuls feasting on your seeds,
    are you red and hairy like Esau,
    are your flowers good in bowls of curried pottage,
    are you a tree of red silk cotton,
    bombax malabarica?

Were you a thousand scented pillars
    around the forecourt of an emperor,
    are you malleable in the whittler's palm,
    are you swooning-pale and infant-smooth,
    are you a parasite tethered to roots of others,
    are you *sandalwood*?

Are you loose-tethered, a yielder of leaves to wind,
    are you a sender-out of roots, are you clone,
    is a forest of your kind a single sentience,

and in fall are you quivering yellow,
boreal, afflicted with melancholy,
a breather of mists and cold,
are you *quaking aspen*?

Do your flowers steam with fragrance as the heat increases,
do the chrysomelids rut within your clutch of petals,
do your blossoms shatter as the beetles copulate,
are you Amazonian—are you *annona sericea*?

Are you a kingdom, are you castles in the air,
are you a garden of Babylon in mist,
are your branches colonies of dreaming epiphytes,
are the flicking tails of lizards lost inside your cities,
are you flying above the prayers of the Maori,
are you *kauri*, the tree that must forgive?

Were you as dense and black as mythic thrones of Hades,
were you strong, were you midnight ripped in lengths,
were you foretelling gleams—Victoria's jet beads—
were you heavier than the fat man's coffin,
were you Pharoah's favorite chair,
are you *ebony*?

Are you dawn redwood or frangipani,
are you whistle thorn or cannonball,
are you linden, myrtle, jacaranda,
are you sourwood or silverbell,
are you a branch of good and evil,
are you the lemurs' Ravenala,
are you Yggdrasil, axis of nine worlds,
are you a cross whose branches reach forever,
are you water-tapping, cloud-catching, sun-devouring,
are you leaf, are you branch, are you root, are you tree?

A Tree for Ezekiel

First of all, know this: the tree was dead,
It had already been dead for a time,
It was going to be dead a long while.
It was a stick in labyrinths of sand.
And yet, and yet—for one Ezekiel,
The dry-bone tree was clothed in chrysolite,
So that the leaves made glitterings in sun.
The bole was swathed in strips of China silk,
The twigs were mummied in gem-colored threads,
The shriveled root began to drink from earth.
A gust came from the East: the sound of wings,
And leaves turned in the wind—blue leaves and green
Looking, and each shaped like a human eye.
A dew arose from earth and bloomed as cloud,
Though in the desert, this was very strange
To see, and also there was far tumult
As if the dunes had changed to waterfalls.
The priest Ezekiel discerned a form
Among the staring blue and green of leaves,
Prismatic figure brightened by the light.
Ezekiel foretold: *Your incense lost,*
Your limestone idols headless in the dust,
Your cities and all of your histories
Wiped from the memories of everyone ...
The centuries forget your name, your love,
The sons and daughters raised from infancy
In years that are themselves forgotten things,
And all there is of comfort is this tree,
Mysterious and riddling-strange to you,
A rainbow covenant, its promises
Too far away in time for you to see.

Ship of Trees

Nails tingle in boards, freezing in the grain,
And the whole house struggles to conjure some
Swaying rootedness, rampire and bulwark
Against invader cold and winter's gusts.
Outside, the still-living limbs comb and catch;
Migrant months ago all leaf-freight tumbled
South to mulch—and so this naked writhing
With no green hands to stem the streams of air.
In the heaped bed, your hazel eyes yawn black,
Staring into the night, at pale tossings
Past the windowpanes, as the winds shiver
The glass, playing it like an instrument.
I lie down by your side to whisper how
Inside each weathered length of sawn clapboard,
—More than two centuries old, that harvest—
Sleep rings of years, the memory of trees.
Wood will remember how to stand in brunt
Of freeze and gash of winds, to dance, to tack
Like a grove of chestnuts sailing the breeze,
Bringing the cargo of us to shores of dawn.
And when you drift away from me, I lie
With eyes open to the rule of darkness,
Hearing the cold withdrawing of the nails,
Watching branches sweep the prickles of stars.
Your breath is pulsing on my cheek, and I
Shift closer, pushing away all winter thoughts,
Letting each die, alone, in the chilly room
Like a stranger who lacks my harbored joy.

A May Flower

Dorothy May Bradford drowned in
Provincetown Harbor while the Mayflower
was at mooring, December 7, 1620.

In green-shot bays my sweetheart sleeps;
She pierced the shadow of the boat
And disappeared—still I must keep
My courage safe from fear she floats
With staring eyes into the deeps
Where liquid devils jeer and gloat.

Did sharp-fanged woods spur Dorothy
To drink up death? No way to gloss
Over trials, nowhere to flee ...
Her heart could augur only loss.
Whoever thought the changing sea
Would alter *crossing* into *cross*?

We pilgrims in the wilderness
Must curb our fancy's imps and ghosts—
A penitent, I here confess
To glimpsing her along the coast:
I meant to say, *God's peace and rest,*
But words fall dead when wanted most.

The Bottle Tree

Beyond the burning cotton fields once grew
A bottle tree; my memory won't tell
What flowering plant it was, though I recall
The loose pale blossoms shaking in the wind
And petals dripping on a raked sand yard.
The leaves were ordinary green, burnt
When August dog-days circled round again,
The hound of seasons chasing its own tail.
Ghost-catching bottles heated air to fire,
Killed any leaf or flower jailed in glass—
I'd guess there were some forty on the boughs,
Reflective things that jarred the sun to make
Exploding stars that jabbed into my eyes.
My steps would falter, walking by the place,
And sometimes I would slip beneath and stare
At carnival displays of bottle-bloom—
The glass fired amethyst by too much sun,
The lightly radioactive cobalt glass,
The twinkling rose, pale pinks, a jello green.
A breeze would whistle in and out the mouths:
I liked to think it was the talk of ghosts
Trapped and calling from the antic bottles.
One night a storm cloud roamed across the farm,
Banging screens against unpainted clapboard,
Thrusting chickens backward in mid-scuttle
Across a wind-raked, tumbled sea of sand.
All night we listened to fell gibberings
As sprites and demons lashed the stallion storm
And winds unpinned the crops from neat-hoed rows.
At dawn I staggered, lifted by the gusts,
And found the tree tormented, crooked, crouched.
The ghosts had burst into a wilderness
Of blackgum swamp along the pale dirt road,
Where I could hear them shrilling in the leaves.

The cries made fine hairs hackle at my nape
As I whirled round to stare into the trees,
Then spun again in haunted fright to look
At bottles smashed to lidless, sharp-edged eyes
That threatened body's branching tree of blood,
Glaring and winking from rain-rumpled dirt
As if some Argos monster, peacock-eyed,
Unbottled by a hurricane of ghosts,
Had surfaced from his shallow Southern grave.

In All Her Gleaming Youth, She Said

Dearest Mother, will you blame me
    Because I could not stay?
And will you rail so bitterly
    When all the world is May?

Last night I stood beside the door
    And looked my fill of you—
Until the overflowing store
    Seemed images of rue.

And yet I could not leave his side
    As light and leaf unfurled.
I am the Forest's promised bride—
    We green the springing world.

The Good-bye

Good-bye, my borrowed bits of loveliness,
You necklaces of pomegranate seeds,
You leaf-green shadows clustered in a gem,
You priceless pearl, redeemer of the dust.
Good-bye to my dear husband, children, friends,
For something wilding calls my secret name,
And light and forest overshadow me.
Already beams that slant between the boles
Go sliding through my skin until I shine,
And white-eyed vireos have plucked at leaves
To build my nest among the sycamores.
I wander emerald woods until I tire—
Pursuing still some moving goal in dreams,
I sleep in leaves beside a nacred sea.
The greeny shadows in this land of peace
Are pattering with rain that brings a scent
Of earth—the droplets rise again as cloud,
Foretelling metamorphosis in me.

Acknowledgements

The poems of "The Book of Ystwyth" were composed in honor of a major retrospective of the work of artist Clive Hicks-Jenkins at The Gregynog Gallery. The sequence appeared in *The Book of Ystwyth: Six poets on the art of Clive Hicks-Jenkins*, a publication launched at the opening. The book was a production of the Carolina Wren Press in Durham, North Carolina, and Grey Mare Press in Aberystwyth, Wales, in association with Llyfrgell Genedlaethol Cymru, The National Library of Wales, 2011. Special thanks to Andrew Wakelin and Peter Wakelin.

Grateful thanks is due those who accepted or requested the following poems for first publication:

A May Flower: *qarrtsiluni*

A Tree for Ezekiel: *Mezzo Cammin*

Artifact: *Mezzo Camin*

"Because I Pass, I Pass, While Dreams Remain": *Angle*

Catriona's Plate: Poems at Clive Hicks-Jenkins (*www.hicks-jenkins.com/poems*)

Clock of the Moon and Stars: *The Flea*

Dear Peregrine,: Poems at Clive Hicks-Jenkins (*www.hicks-jenkins.com/poems*)

Green Wednesday: Clive Hicks-Jenkins' Artlog (*www.clivehicksjenkins. wordpress.com*)

Hermitry: Poems at Clive Hicks-Jenkins (*www.hicks-jenkins.com/poems*)

I Heard Their Wings Like the Sound of Many Waters: *qarrtsiluni*

In All Her Gleaming Youth, She Said: *Mezzo Cammin*

In the Shadow of the Jasmine: *Mezzo Cammin*

Interregnum: *Mezzo Cammin*

Lumen Hour: *Angle*

Master Jug and Lady Candlestick: Clive Hicks-Jenkins (*www.hicks-jenkins. com/poems*)

Mirror Tree, Tree Mirror: *Mezzo Cammin*

Puck in Spring: *Mezzo Cammin*

Red Leaves in Green: *The Round Table Review*

Scout Ceremony: *Mezzo Cammin*

Self-portrait as Dryad, no. 7: *qarrtsiluni*

Ship of Trees: *Angle*

That Which Snatches: *Mezzo Cammin*

The Blue Marches: Poems at Clive Hicks-Jenkins (*www.hicks-jenkins.com/poems*)

The Bottle Tree: *Mezzo Cammin*

The Elder Race: *Mezzo Cammin*

The Foliate Head: *Mezzo Cammin*

The Good-bye: *Mezzo Cammin*

The Great Frost: *The Flea*

The Magnolia Girl: *Books & Culture*

The Sheaf of Wheat: *Mezzo Cammin*

The Stone Court: *Mezzo Cammin*

The Substance: *Angle*

To Make Much of Time: *Angle*

Transfiguration: Port City Poets, blog of *The Wilmington Star*, *www.staronline.com*

Wielding the Tree Finder: *qarrtsiluni*

"Transfiguration" is dedicated to the memory of the late poet Rosanne Coggeshall.

"Interregnum" was written for Eileen St Lauren.

Marly Youmans

A South Carolinian by birth, Marly Youmans is the author of novels and poetry collections, as well as several Southern Appalachian fantasies for younger readers. Her awards include The Michael Shaara Award for *The Wolf Pit* (Farrar, Straus & Giroux, 2001) and The Ferrol Sams Award for *A Death at the White Camellia Orphanage* (Mercer University Press, 2012.) Currently she is serving as a judge for The National Book Award in young people's literature.

Recent and forthcoming books of poetry are *The Throne of Psyche* (Mercer, 2011) and *Thaliad*, an epic poem forthcoming from Phoenicia Publishing in Montreal. Her P. S. Publishing novel, *Val/Orson* (2009), was chosen "Book of the Year" by John Wilson, editor of Books & Culture, who has called her "the best-kept secret among contemporary American writers".

thepalaceat2.blogspot.com

Clive Hicks-Jenkins

Clive Hicks-Jenkins has been called by Simon Callow 'one of the most individual and complete artists of our time'. His work is held in all the principal public collections in Wales and his artist's books with the Old Stile Press are in libraries worldwide. He exhibits regularly with the Martin Tinney Gallery in Cardiff.

His sixtieth-birthday retrospective exhibition at the National Library of Wales in 2011 was accompanied by two publications. The first was an anthology of 27 poems by American and British poets, *The Book of Ystwyth: Six Poets on the Art of Clive Hicks-Jenkins* (Carolina Wren Press), featuring Dave Bonta, Callum James, Andrea Selch, Catriona Urquhart, Damian Walford Davies and Marly Youmans. The second was a major study, *Clive Hicks-Jenkins* (Lund Humphries), with essays by among others Simon Callow, Kathe Koja and Marly Youmans.

www.hicks-jenkins.com